WOMEN LEAD

Heels Are Optional

ISBN: 978-1-7345099-5-3

DEDICATION

This book is dedicated to every little girl who dreams big; keep dreaming.

ACKNOWLEDGEMENT

A special thank you to the women who collectively and selflessly shared their stories:

Nicole Johnson

Dr. Candus Jack

Tammie M. Lilly

Melinda Duplichan, LMSW

Andrea Francis, CRMA/CPT, CYC-p

Dr. LaTracey McDonald

Lynette Edwards

Table of Contents

INTRODUCTION

Someone asked the question: What happens to little girls who dream? The answer is simple; they become women who lead. Those little girls who dream without wavering grow up to influence a generation.

Some choose a path of wealth and renewed mindset while others invest time into reinventing themselves in an effort to become a leading lady amongst their peers.

Licensed professionals, media moguls, PhD graduates, entrepreneurs, educators, authors, songwriters, entertainers, lawyers, film-makers, doctors, engineers, campaign managers, journalists, CEOs, corporate gurus, and influencers are making waves not merely by being women but because they have the skill-set and knowledge it takes to lead.

Women today are not always held to a lower standard than their male counterparts, instead women are shattering glass ceilings. Women are proving that while cooking in the kitchen and caring for children was once the way of life, it is now an option.

Women have fought for the right for equal pay and the right to be seen beyond high heels and make up. Women don't wish to be more than, but equal to, their male counterparts.

Women across the country are taking the bricks once thrown at them and building their own empires. They are taking a lifestyle that once only existed in their dreams and manifesting it to a reality that their daughters may one day be proud of.

Women are leading but not just in the workplace; women continue to lead in communities across the world. Women are advocating for the right to vote, fighting for an equal justice system, and paving the way for more females to reach the top.

Women are not just wearing crowns but passing them to the sisters that sit beside them and challenging them to do better, live better, and more importantly, be better. Be a better sister, friend, mother, and lover; be a calm in the midst of the storm.

Women are the backbone of not only the family but the bedrock of what this world desperately needs; women are leading; high heels are now optional.

Sit back, relax, and enjoy the stories of seven women who have found their voices. Voices that they use to impact their communities, families, and those little girls who dream to one day lead.

.

Boss Mom, the Grind Doesn't Stop and
Neither Do I'

-Nicole Johnson

THE AMERICAN DREAM?

Growing up, my dad always told me that I could do anything that I put my mind to. As a child, *anything* was still very limiting for me because of what I was exposed to on a daily basis. I saw my parents, stepparents, and the rest of the village that had a hand in raising me, working a job. The majority of them were college educated, but regardless, they all seemed to follow the same pattern. They graduated high school, most went on to college while others may have gotten a trade or they went straight into the workforce. Each one of them eventually entered into the workforce, started a family, purchased a home, vehicle, and other high-ticket items then worked tirelessly to support their lifestyle.

For me, I continued to hear the sound of my dad's voice saying, *I could do anything*. However, I knew that whatever journey I pursued, I would still follow a similar pattern as my elders, and so my journey began.

When I was young, I remember spending a lot of time with my paternal grandparents. My grandfather had retired from working for the railroad company and was a small farmer. My grandmother was a stay-at-home mother, who never worked outside of the home, but did a fabulous job of taking care of her household. It seemed like she was always cooking because from breakfast to lunch to dinner, there was always a fresh, hot meal coming out of her kitchen. I can vividly remember on Sunday mornings on our way to church, we would make a pit stop at my grandparents' house to grab a pork roast sandwich, which was fresh out of the oven. Then we would stop by after church, just a couple of hours later, to enjoy her wonderful Sunday spread with all of our immediate and extended family. This is where I learned a lot about the elders of my family.

Of course my grandparents all lived the retired lifestyle. My mom worked for the telephone company, a career that she started while in college and had steadily been growing within the company for many years. My dad graduated in education and became a teacher but would eventually go on to become a guidance counselor, assistant, and then principal during his tenure with the school board. There were other educators within my family and also those within law enforcement. My oldest brother was a truck driver and my sister started climbing the infamous corporate ladder after her college graduation. Every single one of them are Godly, decent, hard-working individuals who I aspired to be just like. Disclaimer: none of us are perfect people and we certainly are all flawed, but we are a family built on love, and love conquers all! The blessing of growing up in such a stable black family is what grounded me to be a strong Johnson woman, and I knew that I wanted to shine my light. For me, I knew that I was going to grow up and become successful.

Both of my parents really valued education and hard work. My dad always refers to a story of my grandfather not supporting his decision to go to college because my grandfather wanted him to follow his path of working for the railroad and on the farm. Begrudgingly, my dad did those things during the summer when he was not in school, but my dad desired to go to college. He still brags now that he went to college on a full sports scholarship, pledged a fraternity, graduated college in three and a half years and went back for two separate master's degrees. My dad would always say that my grandfather never really acknowledged his success until he received his principalship. Once my grandfather visited my dad at work, he realized that my dad ran the whole school.

My mom, on the other hand, went to college but did not finish. She received an opportunity to jump start her career and pursued that option. My mom was (and still is) a hustler! In addition to her job, she loved (and still does) all things crafty. She made most of my clothes and hair bows. She also embroidered and made decorations. Handmade crafts have been her lifelong hobby. She worked her full-time job and hustled on the side. I would often hear my mom talking to my stepdad about business ideas that she had and how much money she had earned doing something that she enjoyed. Her craft business was small, but it was sustainable. She poured her time and energy into making her hobby a successful business.

Because of what my parents modeled for me, I wanted them to be proud of what I did with my life. I always wanted to honor them by making the right decisions and staying true to my morals and values. Although sometimes I fell short, the examples they displayed have always resonated in my mind, still to this day.

I appreciate the "American Dream" my parents demonstrated for me: go to school, make good grades, get a good job, work within your career field, buy the house on the hill with the white picket fence, get old and retire. But somehow along the way, I realized that dream was flawed. The dream kept everyone on this hamster wheel: in debt, struggling to make ends meet, no freedom and always complaining about the job that they dedicated their lives to. My dad always joked about having to 'rob Peter to pay Paul'. Growing up, I thought that was a part of the dream; however, it was not really appealing to me. I wanted more. I wanted freedom. I desired to live a life beyond anything my family had ever modeled for me. Part of my problem was that I did not want to disappoint them. They did their very best to shield me from life's troubles and taught me what I needed to live a *good* life; but deep down my heart desired more.

I must admit that in school, I was not the best student, but I did put on a big front. I did just enough to make my parents proud. They were proud of a 'B' student, so that is what I strived for, sometimes maybe even a 'C'. I did enough to graduate. I went through the motions of school, but I enjoyed the weekends the most. I always envisioned myself having a grand job that afforded me many opportunities in life but never realized that I had to do the work in school to get there. When I was a senior in high school, I got into a program that allowed me to go to school half a day and gain work experience by working the other half of my school day at a business site secured through my high school. I only signed up for the program because I only had to attend school for half of the day, which was very appealing to me. All of the students in this program had to take a business elective that taught them about operations, management, and finance. That elective was where the seeds of business ownership began to be planted within me. Also, the business that I was assigned to was our parish school board office in the technology department. The director would assign me to various tasks from setting up stations within the schools to researching different software. I would then present them to the director who decided which ones to buy based on the school's needs. Every time I presented to her or when she and I would work with the teachers, teaching them about the computer stations and the software, she always told me that I would become a teacher. Because the American Dream, as I knew it, was not interesting to me, becoming a teacher did not sound attractive at all to me. However, later on in life, I did realize that I am called to teach, it is one of my God-given spiritual gifts! I am forever grateful for that high school experience. It allowed me to shift from the mindset of a young lady who could be a loyal unhappy employee to the mindset of a woman who could one day lead beyond the walls of an office.

I navigated through college the same as I did high school. I enjoyed the party life and socializing but I just went through the motions of school. I did not follow in my dad's footsteps of graduating in three and a half years. I graduated proudly, in five years. During college, my sister introduced me to *Rich Dad, Poor Dad*, a book that got me interested in financial freedom. It was as though an entire world had opened for me. The mere thought that I could live a life of freedom and never have to worry about money again gave me hope. Although I did not act upon the principles of that book immediately, my mindset was expanding and the possibilities for me were opening up even more.

The semester I graduated from college, hurricanes Katrina and Rita hit Louisiana. Both hurricanes were catastrophic, and the government stepped in to provide a lot of assistance for our state. I immediately got a job after college working for FEMA to assist with the disaster relief efforts. I remember when I graduated college, I was working at a hotel making $6.66/hour; when I got on with FEMA, I was making over $30 an hour working 12 to 16-hour days. Within my first 6 months, I received several raises and promotions that led me to move a few hours away to New Orleans. Everything was fast paced, and I was making bank! The downfall of it all was that I hated my job because it was extremely stressful. To top it off, I was in a toxic relationship and all of my family was miles away. They were proud of me and encouraged me to work hard and grow in my career. I had enough money to really do whatever my heart desired, yet I was miserable.

For a little entertainment in my life, I started working as a part-time distributor for a *fun party* company. You know, the type of fun party that promotes products that buzzzzzz in the night! It was a sex toy company. These fun parties were booked by groups of women for various occasions and most of them happened within their homes. I would travel to their location, set up my display and sell them items based on their needs and desires, and make a percentage of all of the items that I sold. I really enjoyed my part-time hustle. I was making money and it was an appealing outlet for me to escape my reality.

After a couple of years of really excelling at my hustle, I started getting burned out and I also realized that the sexy conversation was really not my style. Looking back, the experience made me realize that I had that same hustle in me as my parents did, but this hustle was not true to me. I did not feel like that would make my parents proud of me. This hustle slowly buzzzzed away!

About that same time, our state recovered from the hurricanes and the recovery efforts came to an end. I eventually moved back home and got out of that toxic relationship, once and for all. One of my best friends from college helped me secure a job at a healthcare agency, where she was the director. I was hired as the training coordinator and I was responsible for training all of the staff within the agency. At this job, I became a CPR instructor and started my career in corporate training. Unfortunately, I was quickly terminated from the job, as I was from all of the jobs that I acquired over the next few years. I was stuck living the American Dream and I was not fulfilled. However, each time I was fired from yet another healthcare agency, I always had my CPR training skills to fall back on.

The lady who trained me to become a CPR instructor would always tell me about other instructors who were making good money running their own CPR training business. During one of my unemployment periods, the light bulb went off. I realized I could run a CPR training business the same way I ran my fun party business. I would travel to the consumer's location to conduct the training class, which was not the traditional way in the training industry. Traditionally, the training company had a brick and mortar location and the class participants would be trained at that location. However, I knew from my time working at a few agencies that it was a lot of work to get the staff to
travel for the CPR training. I realized that if my business was mobile, it would be more beneficial for my clientele.

Once I realized my business idea could actually work, I started networking and finding out about local government resources for small businesses. I received a lot of assistance designing my business and executing the tasks needed to make my business a reality. I took a leap of faith and never looked back.

Once I started my part-time training business, I was determined to take my time and dedicate myself to building the life I wanted. I wanted my part-time business to ultimately become my full-time business. Because I was not a really good employee, I found more security in business ownership. I did not have the same mindset as I did before and a lot of my family and friends doubted my efforts, but I kept pushing forward. Every time I hit a roadblock, my dad encouraged me to use my degree and go get another job but I remember always crying to my sister that I did not want to work for anyone else. I really wanted to work for myself and I was willing to sacrifice material gains for my freedom and to make financial independence a reality. I knew I had a calling on my life, and I was up for the challenge.

I applied all of my skill sets and became consistent, confident, and careful with every decision along the way. After a few short years, I began to see the fruits of my labor. I was able to run my business full time, eliminating any outside employment and I was in full control of my life. I was starting to gain the freedom I so desperately desired to have, and that motivated me to keep going and apply pressure. The *Rich Dad, Poor Dad* book also taught me that there was a difference between being self-employed and creating a true business system that could run without my presence and create passive income. That has become the goal for my training business and all of my business ventures. A goal that I am still pursuing.

Moreover, I reconnected with a childhood friend, who is now my life partner. At the very beginning of our journey, we became interested in gardening and self-sufficiency, which led us to become Louisiana Master Gardeners. We also completed a beginning farmers' training program through Louisiana State University. We are currently in our second season of farming and have ownership in a local farmers market in a food desert within our city. We desire to buy property where we can live and farm. We desire to leave a legacy for our family that includes being self-sufficient, having the ability to provide our own food for our family. We want to instill the skills of our ancestors and rebuild our cultural practices.

Shortly after my partner and I reconnected, we had a baby. With everything going on in my life, I was now a mother to a son, an African American son. The birth of my son redefined my entire life course and everything that I had planned. In the beginning, I simply wanted to create a life for myself where money was not a factor. I could travel, serve my community, and help build those around me. Having a son gave me a sense of urgency in my efforts, and soon, generational wealth took on a whole new meaning. The most important part of my journey is not only providing a meaningful life for my son but also ensuring my legacy can be handed down to him. I know how it is to live someone else's dream; therefore, I want my son to witness all that I am and build upon that.

Financial freedom and wealth are what I strive to pass on. The ability to navigate through this world without the burden or the lack of financial mobility will be a game changer for my son. Financial freedom means that my son will not have to compromise his dignity and pride for a paycheck. He will have the ability to write the blueprint for his very own version of the American Dream.

As a boss mom, I have learned that the American Dream still exists; the meaning is just different for me. Like my dad, I evolved from what the generation before me completed, and I really wanted a life that was truly free. In my opinion, entrepreneurship equates to freedom. I am free to be creative at all times and I do not have the limitations set forth by employers. Being an entrepreneur allows me to try my hand at all sorts of things, gain momentum, and secure revenue. Regardless of the outcome, each business venture has contributed to my success. When asked what advice I would give to new entrepreneurs, I encourage them to DREAM BIG!

I cannot credit anyone more than God for directing the path of my life. It is my faith in God that continues to give me the courage to take advantage of all of the opportunities that are presented to me. My dream may differ from yours and that is perfectly fine. What matters most is that we keep dreaming until the day arrives to live out the dreams placed in our hearts. Regardless of where you are on your journey, remember that you can have it all; the business, the family, the house on the hill with the white picket fence; you can have your own American Dream!

About the Co-Author

Nicole Ryane Johnson is a business management graduate from the University of Louisiana at Lafayette. She is a serial entrepreneur, having ownership in several business ventures, including CPR 2 Geaux, Certification Connect, L4S Farms, Fightingville Fresh Farmers Market and Fightingville Fresh Growers' Collective. She has a passion for teaching and encouraging others in the areas of entrepreneurship, farming, and self-sustainability.

Nicole is the mother of a two-year old son, Treyson Roy. He keeps her on her toes, but she manages to juggle everything that comes her way. Along with her life partner, Travonic, they strive to raise their son in love and plan to model a life of financial freedom for Treyson.

Nicole enjoys networking with other like-minded individuals. She is a boss by day and a mom by night who is learning daily that the American Dream is exactly what you make of it.

'The Key to the Core has Already Been Provided. It is Our Choice to Use it.'

-Dr. Candus Jack

MANIFESTATION THROUGH MOVEMENT

"Move," was consistently uttered from the small still voice in my ear. How to move and where to move was questionable to me. I kept hearing it repeatedly. It was unshakable because at that time, I was unmovable…until I found myself in a position where I needed to turn to God to search for answers...yet again.

At that time in my life, I had accomplished great things. I had just graduated with my doctorate's degree, was in a committed relationship with the man I eventually married, and I had time on my hands to recover from four years of doctoral studies. From the perspective of individuals on the outside looking in, it appeared that everything was great. Why not? The perfect timeline in my head showed that once I completed my studies, I would have time to pursue a relationship and things would fall into place. Ironically, just as things seemed to be great, I began to feel this huge void in my spirit.

I did not feel the way I envisioned I would. I thought I would feel free and relieved after dedicating four years of discipline and hard work to school. Yet, when things began to slow down, I not only felt unhappy, I felt empty. The word "move" greeted me again. I was so confused. I was so wrapped up in my own misery and timeline for new opportunities to develop that I was unable to embrace the people and experiences along the way. Let me explain.

The fear of incompletion had always been a part of my journey in the past. I would even dream about not completing my master's degree or not accomplishing important goals. My fears led me to becoming a perfectionist, which really complicated things. There is a message in this. I began to task towards finite goals I developed instead of becoming aware of God's purpose for my life. Although God helped me fulfill many goals, I was unfulfilled.

I noticed that for many years of my adult life, I lived in a pattern. Any time I experienced disappointment or pain I hid behind work. I would either get a second job, start a business project, or enroll in school. It appears that I was trying to escape from the pain I felt and it seemed to be the most logical thing to do. Why? Because it was productive. As years went by, I realized that productivity could only get me so far. I needed divine fulfillment. I compare it to drinking a bottle of water after an intense workout instead of a can of Coke. Coke tastes good, but water is the only liquid that would quench my thirst. I was in need of a consistent supply of living water.

Since I was a child, I was always a lover of God, but at times, my relationship with Him became part-time as I got older. I allowed work to take precedence over Him, not because I wanted to, but because my stubbornness and lack of wisdom allowed work to consume me. Nonetheless, God has been trying to get my full and undivided attention for many years. He called me to become someone greater than my imagination could lead me to become. Abiding by His will was the only way I would be able to walk in that purpose. In the past, I didn't listen. But I'm now grateful He never stopped pursuing me.

I've gone through a lot of hardships in the past, including a nasty custody battle. I often wonder if my experiences were God's way of getting my full attention. I wasn't a rebellious person or one to live irresponsibly, so I was bothered by the events that took place in my life. I asked some of the same questions many people ask such as, "Why me? How did this happen? What did I do to deserve this?" When I did not get the answers and when things got worse, I knew what I faced was beyond what I could do. I felt helpless, challenged, and confused.

As God began to reveal Himself to me through other circumstances, I began to trust Him more. I eventually began to journal my blessings in remembrance of His goodness. That helped me cope when my father was diagnosed with cancer. During that time, I just knew God would heal him. My faith was super strong and my focus, next to raising my son, was to ensure my father was safe and that he received the care he needed. Although I was extremely optimistic during that time, I faced more disappointment.

In less than 1 year, his battle with cancer ended. Can you recall a time in your life when you trusted God for something, but felt let down? That was exactly how I felt. I was devastated initially and felt that once again, everything was so wrong…until the day of his funeral. God gave me so much peace that it seemed unreal. My perspective changed in that moment. He healed my father by taking him into heaven. I learned that if what we want in life does not align with His will, we will find disappointment each time things don't align with our plans. My father suffered during his battle with cancer and although I did not want to lose him, knowing he was rejoicing in heaven helped me rejoice in the Lord.

I continued to hold on to my faith in God and persevere. I completed my studies, received elevation at work and committed to a relationship. Things I hung on my vision board were manifesting, yet I was still unhappy. It was eye opening to discover for myself that things don't bring us joy; God does. He helped me grow academically, but I was a spiritual novice. I'm proud of my success, but ambition and drive for success and tangibles don't supersede the abundance we get from an intimate relationship with God. Just when I began to connect with my feelings, the sound of God's voice became more distinct. *"Move,"* He said. I began to hear it more consistently, and then I heard, *"write."* This was so foreign to me. I wondered, "Write what and why?" After graduating, in my mind, I retired from writing. It had to be my imagination.

You may recall moments when you did not obey God because you felt what He was urging you to do did not make sense. In doing so, as believers, we risk missing opportunities to step out on faith and allow God to catapult us forward. God's persistence grew, and once I allowed myself to listen to Him and actually reflect on what He was telling me to do, it hit me. I was in a great place in my life, but I felt a heavy weight holding me back. I was physically tired, frustrated with work, and emotionally drained. God revealed to me that I allowed certain events from my past to hold me hostage. As I stated before, I hid behind work. I never dealt with my feelings from the past nor released those burdens to God because I did not realize any existed! I allowed embarrassment, injustices I faced, and fear to isolate me from opportunities and people because I buried myself in work. I was not allowing myself to live freely. God revealed it was time for me to share my testimony.

God hears our cries and He answers us. Instead of trusting His timing, we often search for details and try to rationalize things in our heads rather than just hear and obey Him. I've always wanted to share my testimony, but I waited for the fairy tale ending to do so. Because my story did not end that way, I felt others would not be blessed by it. God showed me that through writing, I was not only able to share my testimony, but help others live in faith, peace, and joy even if life's outcomes do not currently match our desires.

Movement also revealed that circumstances typically don't change unless we pour into others. This takes our minds off ourselves and helps us love unconditionally. We're often deceived with the misconception that things in our lives must be nearly perfect before we can make positive contributions to society. 2 Corinthians 5:7 states that we must walk by faith and not by sight. In order to see movement, we must be willing to move.

Writing was not a passion of mine and I never envisioned myself writing a book. In fact, I never envisioned pouring into ministry the way I do currently. When we trust God, He will reveal talents and take us places beyond our imagination. I would have never written the word author next to my name, but God did. After several months of pondering on how I would construct my first book, He revealed to me the fruit of the spirit.

I began to write. The moment I began to "move" (write), God began to provide me with wisdom. When we spend too much time wavering in life, we will eventually miss our window of grace. The moment we decide to move through courage, God will reveal more than we could imagine on our own. Within a couple of months, more than half of my book was written, then I stopped writing to plan my wedding. After the wedding, the urge to write again returned. In addition, I knew I had to complete this assignment and not allow distractions to take place, so I continued to write. Just when things in my life seemed to make sense, and I began to become comfortable with where I was and become optimistic about my future, the enemy rushed in like a flood and attacked my marriage.

All I could think about was completion…again among so many other things. I won't lie. These thoughts entered my mind, "Why is there always a new problem? Why can't my life be normal?" In that season, God's beauty was revealed. Had He not pursued me years ago, it's possible I would have given up during difficult times. I couldn't help but think that the enemy was trying extremely hard to hold me back and that God had great plans for my life. Then it hit me. God has been preparing me to withstand the attack of the enemy for several years. In the past, when I thought I was alone, He was with me. When I thought I couldn't hear Him, He spoke. When I was confused, He guided me. Writing my book was not only to help me heal from my past, but to equip me with biblical knowledge to help me prepare for what was ahead and to share that knowledge with others. The more I learned about spiritual fruit, the easier it was for me to not only love my husband despite our early marital hardships, but to also love God so much that I fought even when I felt uncomfortable. In this process, God revealed the deeper side of love.

The enemy used every tactic to block me from my purpose, but God had the final say. You may have experienced a long waiting season and just when things appeared to be hopeful, new problems occurred. When we understand how angry the enemy becomes when we commit to God's will, we'll realize he will do all he can to prevent us from obtaining our promise. Knowing this gives us fuel to fight back in the supernatural rather than the natural.

I encourage each person in this position to move with faith. Through each of my struggles, God allowed *The Core: Exercising Godly Character Through the Nourishment of Spiritual Fruit* to manifest. This book is about the fruit of the spirit, "love, joy, peace, forbearance, kindness, goodness, faithfulness, gentleness and self-control" (Galatians 5:22-23), which helps believers discover who we were created to become in Christ through transformation. Through my struggles, I had to grow to give God the glory. God has been trying to produce something through me that I never acknowledged—creativity and the love for ministry. Had I not listened to God's initial "move", I would have never discovered His power that is still within me.

It's okay to strive to achieve things in life, but it's hard to appreciate them if we don't strive to become better people in Christ. In doing so, we must know what God's expectations of us are. The upside-down character of the world leads us to false representations of who God called us to become. The world paints the picture that love is based on conditional things and that our worth is based on popularity and the amount of affirmations we receive. The world also equates joy with happiness and peace with being problem-free. When we realize what God's expectations are, then we can truly adhere to them and discern between living a righteous life rather than living under the unrighteous commands of man.

God was showing me what life is about. He showed me how to live freely and abundantly. He helped me let go of things that weighed me down and cast them unto Him. When I was able to do so, I was able to approach disappointment and discomfort differently than I did previously. I was also able to become more attentive to who He created me to become in Christ.

Interestingly, I published my second book a year later. Although I thought my writing was complete after my first book, God led me to another one. I almost fought the idea initially but felt a huge conviction each time I publicly stated that I was not a writer. The bible states that life and death is in the power of the tongue (Proverbs 18:21). What we say we either can't or don't want to do can be the very thing God called us to do. What is God speaking into your heart? Have you asked God what your purpose is? I learned to seek God for what He wanted for my life rather than just petition my own desires.

2 Corinthians 13:11 states, "Aim for restoration, comfort one another, agree with one another, live in peace; and the God of love and peace will be with you." I am a firm believer that we were created to live a character aligned with who God is and help each other in love. We

are privileged to live in such a beautiful world through God's love, yet society displays little appreciation through divisive mannerisms and selfishness. Because of it, when life knocks us down, we seek answers in the natural through desperation. The manifestation of my second book and devotional was to promote awareness and encourage people to live in the spirit each day. It shows what self-control looks like during a heated argument, what excellence looks like in a workplace that's not providing basic needs, how to love yourself when others no longer do and so much more. I've had to learn to fight the good fight of faith (1 Timothy 6:12) rather than place faith in myself to lean on my own understanding.

I continue to minister the word of God to share with people how to live freely each day. Through struggles, knowing people care is fuel to help us progress forward. And that's just it. As long as we don't stop moving, we will experience great things. I moved through faith, nonstop prayers for myself and others, listening, learning more about the word of God and obedience. It helped me develop courage, confidence, love, peace, joy and the ability to stretch in ways unimaginable. Movement never stops and God also allows us to move through a place of being still. Once I began to replace busy with rest in God, fulfillment found me along with many opportunities.

About the Co-Author

Dr. Candus, a native of Beaumont, TX, currently residing in Houston, TX, has a mission to help people center their lives in Christ. She is known for *The Core: Exercising Godly Character Through the Nourishment of Spiritual Fruit,* her Christian book about the fruit of the spirit. She wrote it to help people apply knowledge of God each day. Her personal journey and relationship with God prompted her to write Christian books and encourage individuals to strengthen their faith. Her goal is to inspire individuals through her personal testimony that through God all things are possible.

Additionally, she wrote *The Core of Everyday Life* as a spinoff devotional book and journal from *The Core: Exercising Godly Character Through the Nourishment of Spiritual Fruit*, to encourage people to become intentional about their spiritual journey and relationship with God each day. She believes that the more time we devote to God, the stronger our core becomes, leading to spiritual transformation. She also understands the importance of spending time with family, rest, wellness and enjoying life.

Dr. Candus is a motivational speaker and aims to counsel individuals to show them ways to apply knowledge of God despite their circumstance. Most importantly, she wants to send a message that regardless of what people experience in life, they can overcome any obstacle through faith in God. She recently founded *Core Refined* in 2020 to encourage men and women to become centered in Christ. She is available via the Dr. Candus handle on various social media platforms including Instagram, Facebook, Twitter and YouTube. To learn more about *Core Refined,* and how to purchase her books, please visit https://drcandus.wixsite.com/core.

'Finding Peace in the Valley'

-Tammie M. Lilly

WHO AM I?

I am a mother of three beautiful children, each beautiful in their own way, each having their own identity with their very own expressions. I am a pastor's wife. It has been a learning experience, but I enjoy the fact that the package came with five exceptional children, one of which is the same age as me, and three grandsons. I am a business owner, but most importantly, I am a child of God. Just recently I have embarked on this journey of being an author. I have written one e-book, one paperback book, and a book collaboration which is a collection of prayers, devotionals, and declarations.

I started this journey of being an author to solidify my income tax company. I attended an event and the host talked about being an author, something I had never thought I wanted. The host gave examples about business owners, people in ministry, and other authors being able to solidify themselves as an expert in their field by writing a book. I quietly listened as the words rolled around in my head. One day, I finally decided that I was going to add authorship to my list of titles. I took an article I wrote a few years ago and turned it into an e-book that I give away. Afterwards, I started my second book about my field. To fund this project, I started pre-selling my book.

I could have never anticipated the doors that are continually opening up for me as an author. With the book collaboration, I gained the title of Amazon's best-selling author. I have been invited to be on different platforms. I have been mentioned in several publications. I feel privileged and honored to be able to be used by God, and I think because of the guidance of the Holy Ghost or Holy

Spirit, whatever you want to use in this manner, that I might enhance and better the lives of others. I know that because of the compassion that I show others, God is opening doors that can't be closed and closing doors that can't be open.

I own a company by the name of KRC Tax and Business Services. I have been in the income tax industry for 20 years, but I have been an entrepreneur since 2012. I decided to be an entrepreneur in the field that I love so much because I got tired of seeing companies mistreat their customers. They treat them like they mean nothing when they are one of the most important assets of their business.

I believe that God is beginning to open more doors for me. These doors began opening when I married my current husband. He is a pastor and a much older gentleman. Because he was a seasoned pastor, he guided me in my spirituality. When you know God's voice, which is His words, you recognize when you are out of His will. You know how to see what your purpose is. You can see your destiny clearer. You are not confused about if you should go to the left or right. At that moment I knew that I was supposed to do more to solidify my business with my writing, and also to tell my story. I was supposed to tell my testimony to bless others who may be going through or have experienced a trial that they don't think they can ever recover from.

As a woman of God, I try to treat everybody with Biblical principles and morals. I work to uphold my integrity no matter who the person is, their background, nor their money. Owning my business allows me the ability to be me. And I really enjoy that. I get to go to bed every night knowing that I am making a positive impact on the world. I sleep with ease and don't have to worry about what I have done throughout the workday. I do not have to worry if what I have done will come back on me in a negative manner.

I am an Overcomer

Biggest Hurdle: Throughout my life, I have overcome a lot by the grace of God. Children in most cases grow up with their mothers in their lives. Parents are there to feed, protect, care, guide, and love their children.

At the age of 11, I lost my mother. It happened on a Saturday during the Thanksgiving season. We were supposed to be going to Dallas for the high school football playoffs. We never made it. Although my mother was in good physical health, she had some health issues and had some bad habits, which many of us have. Some have bad eating habits, drinking, smoking, etc. God saw it as the time to call her home.

That age is a critical stage in a child's life; some people can say that they really needed their mother. This was no different with me and my mother. Well honestly, we will always need our mothers. You know no man knows the day or the hour that they will leave this earth. She left this world and left me and my brother behind. I was not asked if I wanted to keep my mother. I was not asked if I wanted to go with my mother. She just left.

So, I guess in life you have things that happen to you that you have no control over. I'd like to think that I am an overcomer because the odds were stacked against me, a motherless child out here in this unkind world. But by the grace of God!

With the death of my mother, I learned exceedingly early how to accept things that I cannot change. Things that are happening that I can change, those are things that I make the effort to make changes in. But the things that I know that I cannot change, I have learned to accept them for what they are. I guess you can say early on I learned an especially important life lesson.

After the passing of my mother, I did not have the happiest childhood, but I dealt with it. I knew that trouble did not last always. I knew that one day I would not have to endure the things that I was dealing with then. That is a whole book and I will make sure it gets told. Despite all the turmoil, God is so good.

So, when I think about the things that I overcame that is the first major obstacle that comes to mind. I have dealt with failed relationships in my life such as a divorce. I knew that if I passed the test of losing a mother, I would make it through. This wouldn't be a walk in the park, I still battled through and survived it.

Expectation of a Healthy Son: I can remember like it was yesterday carrying my joy, but something went wrong. My son unexpectantly came early; he was premature and underdeveloped. Mistakes were made and I was told that he would not be "normal". But doctors do not have the final say because he was not even expected to make it home. He is my special needs son, and he is now an adult. He is who he is. He cannot do some things, but he can do a lot of things. He is my son, and nothing can change that. My other kids will grow up and leave the nest, but he will not. I am okay with that; I accepted that years ago and I own it.

As I sit here this very moment reflecting on 43 years of life, I realize that over the years, I was just merely living. I surrounded my life around my children. I am getting excited because I am no longer asleep, I have awakened. After the end of my marriage and becoming a single mother, I just went through the motions of life and caring for my children. I had 2 kids from the marriage. I had my youngest while going into another relationship that should not have been.

Time to wake up: All the obstacles have led and prepared me for now. I have had so many wonderful things happen to me in this year. They say it is a pandemic, but I honestly do not see a pandemic. I look at this as a time to shine. If I had a choice, I would have not took the cards that I was dealt. Thank God and now here I am.

WOW—An Author: I am in a position that I would have never ever thought I'd be in. I am an author. I am the child who was never a good reader. I was a child that was never a really good writing composition student. But… here I am now. When I think about an author, I imagine a really good reader. When I think about an author, I think about somebody that can write so beautifully and eloquently. And in school I never was that student. And here I am now. So, this is an overcome moment for me. God has a way of putting you in a position and giving you something that you never thought you would ever have. He has the ability to put you in the position and connect you to people that you need to be successful.

Life is a Gym, Working Out Gets You Stronger

I learned to be strong at a young age because of the death of my mother. The day after I lost my mother, my sister (on my father's side) and I were having a conversation and she told me that I would see my mother again. That statement gave me such comfort. Although in my child like mind, I was thinking soon as in a month or something. My mother has been gone for over 30 years, practically all my life. I have heard people say that they do not know what they would do if they lost their mother or father. I can tell you what you would do, you would live and reflect on the fun memories of your parents, but you would move on because that's part of life. Death is a part of life. Who says that you get the opportunity to keep your parents here forever and the next person does not? If you do not understand that and accept it then you are going to have a hard time dealing with life. Life will deal with you. As people of Faith, you should understand that we are living here on earth temporarily. Understanding this simple fact has made me stronger and gave me the ability to endure. Know that trouble does not last always.

I have a mark on my face from when I fell down the stairs when I was younger. I am no longer bleeding from that fall down the stairs; it does not even hurt anymore, but the mark is still there. Over time, all wounds heal. As it does when we lose a loved one, you still miss them. As a person of faith, you know that it is a part of life. There is nothing you can do about it. You cannot bring them back to life. In life, there are two things you cannot control. When you are born and when you die.

My strength comes from my faith. I have grown more in the last 5 years than I have grown in my whole life. Spirituality comes in play with maturity. Also, with knowledge. The bible tells us, my people perish due to the lack of knowledge. I was dying for years. I was perishing, now I am living. I mean really living. I am awaken and will not slumber again. I want to support. I want to bless and be blessed of course. I know if I am being a blessing, blessings for me will come automatically. I have laid seeds in good ground and my harvest is here. I didn't stop, I am consistently laying more seeds to harvest. I am getting abundant harvest, enough to give away.

Victory Is Mine

What have I had great victory over, I asked myself? Victory is growth for me. Victory each year is evolving to a better version of myself. My victory is my story. My victory is my giving heart. I get tunnel vision on a venture, then I detour to how can I help someone in what I am doing. The Holy Spirit led me to a movement called #supportbegansupport. Although I did not know it, but this has always been my story. I always say, how can you expect a business to flourish? The answer is with someone to support your business. In order for your business to work you must get support. People must buy your product and/or use your services in order for you to have revenue to maintain your business and to maintain your household. A business owner has incredibly unique needs. It is not like you go into your 9 to 5. You do your job and every payday you get paid. For a business owner you have to create your own paycheck.

In the beginning, you wear lots of hats. You are the admin sending out a whole bunch of emails and following up with them. You are the sales team, building a rapport with customers to gain their trust. You are marketing and the finance team. You must make sure you have funds to pay the overhead. So, a business owner's walk is incredibly unique versus being an employee. You need support from others. You have lots of competition in the same industry as you, so you need to sow in good soil to get a good harvest. That is where #supportbegansupport was birthed from. So that is my story #supportbegansupport.

I see people using the social media platform. They use this resource and platforms for destruction. I have chosen to use it to build. I watch the videos. It is like a train wreck and you cannot look away. I just shake my head as I tell myself that I am going to counteract what I see in this world.

This Reason Why I Do What I Do

I have been a mother for 21 years, and I thought my biggest motivation over the years was my children. That's why I named my company KRC Tax and Business Services. KRC are the initials for my children: Kelvin, Rodney, and Claudette. I want my children to look at what their mother has accomplished and know that they are able to do it too. It's my true motivation; my secondary motivation is myself. Helping others, using my God-given talent, my God-given destiny. You know there is an old song that says that I am bringing souls to Jesus by the services that I give. If I bless somebody and I make it very clear that I'm a woman of faith, I'm a Child of God and I give him the glory. This may encourage those that I encounter the motivation to find their faith and put their trust in God. Now that is the ultimate motivation and reward for me.

Impacting Others

My target audience is aspiring and new business owners. I know how I felt when I first started this journey of entrepreneurship. People didn't necessarily understand entrepreneurship; a lot of times they couldn't understand why I wanted to own a business. They thought it was wrong to have that desire. They frowned upon it. Naysayers will ask you when you are going to get a job.

I want to impact those who have that real genuine desire to be an entrepreneur. Those who desire entrepreneurship but do not know what all that entrepreneurship entails. They've heard myths about what it involves. They think you can work whenever you want to. They think it is taking vacations when you want to. They look at the romantic side of being an entrepreneur, and they do not realize it is a lot of work. I strive to impact the business owner, the real, true, die-hard to the heart, business owner. Also, to give awareness to the ones who don't have an understanding of entrepreneurship.

Legacy That I Leave

My legacy is my company. I would like to leave my company to my children. But realistically, they may not even want it. It will be there for them if they opt to carry it on. Then there's my books. I write books that are timeless like *Think and Grow Rich*. This book has been rewritten numerous times and the foundation make royalties off it. I would like to leave this sort of asset for my children. When I heard about this as an option, I knew that this was what I wanted for my legacy. I remember hearing of another example. A woman wrote a book that her son relaunched after she had long left this world. The reality is anyone can fall upon hard times, I want my children to have that alternative. They could always relaunch it and sell it if they fall upon hard times; this could be their rainy-day fund.

So often in the white community, parents and grandparents leave inheritance for the child or children. In the black community, it is believed that there is something wrong with leaving your children something to build on. We feel like we are spoiling the child. In fact, the bible talks about inheritance. One example is the prodigal son. The prodigal son requested his inheritance early, but the point is he had a birthright. There is nothing wrong with leaving my children something behind that they can use. They add to it and their kids add to it and so on. Yes, they have their own minds, their own dreams, and ambitions. And they can have that, and I respect that, but I still want to leave my children something that they can use as an asset to make it their own. So, when asked what my legacy is, I want to leave behind a foundation, something tangible, so they can add onto. My mother, my grandmother, and my grandfather left something behind for me and my brother.

Unfortunately, I did not understand at the time due to the lack of guidance. I did not know how to use it at the time. I did not respect what was left for me and my brother. I didn't value the house at the time. You live and you learn.

That is why I work so hard to teach and guide my children. I have been told by a very wise person that it doesn't matter when the flower blooms, it is still a flower and it smells just as sweet. The bees, butterflies, and other pollinators will still love the sweet nectar.

About the Co-Author

Tammie M. Lilly is a Pastor's wife, mother, business owner, and most importantly a Woman of God. She has excitedly accepted a new title of being an author. She owns KRC Tax & Business Services where they offer tax prep, tax resolutions, bookkeeping and notary services. She has 20 years of experience in the tax industry. In 2012, Tammie decided to start her own company after seeing years of business as usual. Instead of putting value in monetary gain, Tammie understands the customer is the asset and without them, you could not have the revenue. She knew it was her time to allow her light to shine with morals, integrity, and principles. Her book, *Why My Refund Is So Low* helps aspiring and new business owners with their taxes. Taxes require preparation the entire year. When a taxpayer goes from employee to an employer/business owner/entrepreneur, your taxes change. Your income can go up, down, or stay the same, but your taxes do not do what you expect. This book is to save them from the shock of the change.

'Change Happens When People Are Given the Guidance They Need to Draw on Their Own Strength'

-Melinda Duplichan, LMSW

TRANSITION YOUR PAIN INTO PASSION, PROFIT, AND PEACE

"Grieving is intense and it is non-stop intense. Even if things are quiet, and you're sitting there in your chair, kind of staring off into space, inside, the intensity is raging."

~Lori Ennis

Like a musical fugue, the figures of myself pass through me without remorse, switching and changing gears at their own will, not mine. They take their memories with them, dragging the association behind them like a rotted, old tree stump. I feel the weight of their existence in their absence after they go, and as I dream my way from one persona to the other, I wonder who is "they" and who is "me". My perception shifts as I do. These brain fogs, or whatever you want to call them, tie the ends of my days together like an uneven weave of raw linen, ragged yet beautiful.

I try to make it through the day, shuffling from persona to persona, some days managing as one. I feel no fear, for this is the "who's" that I am. I do feel a tightness when I wake from a fog, constricted by the unknowing of the moments I may have missed from my own life, but I pace myself. I transmute my confusion into patience, then freedom, willing my life to carry on "business as usual" even if disjointed by the differing embodiments.

Weaving the day together through awareness of not just "the self" - but all of them, I slowly piece together what makes me who I am, wholly. Not disjointed. Not separated.

But unified. I imagine the idea of a wholly constructed self, as it seems we humans are meant to have, but then I remember my story. No way could I be any other way at this moment; this time. Maybe, someday, my personas will decide to fuse together, and carry time in a straighter line. But for now, my story begs for me to find clarity where I can, amidst my personal brand of confusion.

There's wisdom and lessons hidden amidst the fog, and like raindrops in water, they ripple outwards, echoing through the caverns that have been carved by my many selves. Is anyone there to hear them? Am I? Like workers in a diamond mine, my selves work together to build my life. It's more of a collaborative effort, to be sure, but it's my work. Mine, and mine, and mine, and mine, and mine.

Long before I started to heal from the loss of my son, which was the most intense grief this side of heaven, I attempted to cover my pain with things that numbed me from the outside, but did nothing to heal the inside.

It was easier for me to cope by burying my grief beneath layers of superficial "band-aids" that only covered the hurt but didn't cleanse my wound. I guess it was a way of protecting myself from being able to *feel*.

Those "band-aids" gave me a false sense of control, after feeling like every bit of control had been taken away from me. The sad thing was, my personal band-aids were in the form of numbness and apathy. This was followed by a long season of deep depression, fierce anger, and even feelings of hatred. Emotionally, I pushed people away and closed myself off to any meaningful relationship. For some reason, I felt safer living on the fringes, letting no one get past the surface.

However, my attempts at burying my grief also caused me to lose my sensibility. In turn, I invited so many harmful things into my life—including a harmful relationship that almost killed me. My methods of controlling my emotions and trying to protect myself from further pain actually caused multiple wounds and afflictions in the process.

As I write this, I sense there are many women who are in the same boat—carrying deep hurts, yet working hard to conceal them instead of letting God heal them. I sense there are many who desperately want to leave their pain and grief behind, but feel it is safer to remain in the valley rather than be led into the vulnerability of light. After all, light exposes things—things we might not want exposed. Yet, after a few moments of letting our eyes adjust, we start to see clearer than we've ever seen before.

Even in my darkest hours, as I wore my cloak of depression and carried my dagger of hatred, I knew—*knew*—God was the Ultimate Healer who could restore me to full health inside and out. That tiny mustard-seed of faith was still there and it was *enough*.

Sometimes, all we need to hear is the word *enough*. We need to be reminded that the small spark of hope, the flicker of light, and the tiny seed of faith is enough. Will you say that word aloud? Right where you are, no matter what you're doing, pause and say, "It's enough."

That moment, for me, was when God said, "Melinda, you have started to heal." I was assured that my deeply buried seed of faith had taken root and was starting to grow. The Lord reminded me that even the smallest amount of faith could and *would* move mountains.

Finally, after a long, dark night of the soul, I was ready to step into the light. And as my eyes adjusted to the brightness of hope, I saw a new horizon for the first time in many, many years.

I found myself standing above my valley of death looking toward a new horizon of possibility—endless possibility!

My friend, can you imagine it? Wherever you are, in your own personal valley of hopelessness and defeat, can you look up? There, on the horizon, is a higher place. It's a place that may seem unattainable, but it is definitely within reach! You may not feel like you have the strength to reach it, but with God, you have all the strength you need.

It all begins with a simple prayer: "God, please give me strength and clarity." This was my constant prayer to God starting in August of 2019. And you know what? I have received exactly that—strength and clarity. Before long, that prayer turned into a blessing and I found myself stronger than I'd ever been. It was as if God removed a heavy cloud that had been blocking the sun's rays. And once those rays of light began to shine through, I knew I was finally on the road to success.

Now, keep in mind, it's *okay* not to know all the details moving forward. The important thing is to take the first step. I didn't understand every detail of my newfound freedom, I just knew God had a plan and would work it out in my life. And as I've faithfully put one foot in front of the other, I'm finding that all of my hopes and dreams are coming true.

Even in the midst of this unprecedented time called "2020," I am flourishing like I've never flourished before. And it's all because that mustard seed of faith took root and continues to grow no matter what is going on in the world around me.

I share my story with you because I believe there is something inside of ALL of us that is struggling to get out. It might be a vision of entrepreneurship, a new life venture, or a bold step of faith, but you've pushed it down for so long, you don't know how to let it out. Destructive thoughts circle your mind such as:

I will never change.

I can't possibly achieve that.

Others know my past.

I'm not worthy.

I'll be stuck in this darkness forever.

But listen to me. No matter what thoughts are bombarding you and keeping you from stepping out in faith, believe me when I say, "You CAN do it!" With the tiniest glimmer of hope and the smallest step forward, you can start to heal and move toward your God-given destiny.

After my moment of breakthrough, I became very specific with the Lord in my prayers. I pretty much handed Him a checklist of things I wanted. Not only did I ask Him to guide me in my health, career, and personal achievements, I asked Him to bless me with a Godly man. In fact, here is a short list of things I prayed for in a husband:

- That he would be God-fearing

- That he would be honest and trustworthy

- That he would be someone who would communicate his needs and wants clearly

- That he would be someone who commands his own

- That he would be someone who *knows* Who sits at the head of our table

- That he would be someone who *wants* to be married

You see, I was done with mediocre hopes and dreams. I was done wasting my time on "almost right." I wanted the *exact* person God had in mind for me and I was very specific in my requests.

At that time, I started setting goals for every area of my life. I even gave God a timeline of when I hoped they would be accomplished. Much to my delight, ALL of my requests were heard. Bit- by-bit, my dreams started to become a reality.

Then, in December of 2019, God pressed on my heart to tell my story by writing *Inside of Me*. It is my testimony, my journey, and my perspective. And I cannot not wait to share it with as many people as possible! Once I started writing and sharing other people's stories of pain and triumph, a heavy burden was lifted. I saw clearly the many blessings in my life, and I was able to look back at the roadblocks and see how I stumbled over them. But God picked me back up and gave me a new perspective—a healing perspective.

At the time of this writing, I am only two semesters away from getting my doctorate in social work. I currently have my own business, Zemora Pathways, LLC, and I absolutely love the work I do. What I do is unique. I help others realize their potential and draw them out of their deep pain and depression to help them view life from a different perspective. My heart desires to teach the essentials of life and open doors that have been long closed to health and vitality.

Today, the world is spinning out of control, but I have never been more solid about my life's purpose. It's all because of that tiny mustard seed of faith that remained steadfast in my soul. Once I remembered it was there, I was able to cultivate it and allow God to grow it. And I have no doubt that His blessings will keep coming. He will fulfill my destiny.

About the Co-Author

Melinda is a Licensed Master Social Worker (LMSW), Placenta Encapsulator, and Doula with an office located in Lafayette, Louisiana. Melinda is currently studying to take her Licensed Clinical Social Workers test (LCSW), and final school approval for her Doctorate in Social Work. Melinda is the owner of Zemora Pathways, LLC and has certifications in Sports Social Work, and is completing certification in Sex Therapy. She works with children, young adults, couples, individuals, and families using an eclectic approach tailored to the unique needs of each new client. This is where she cultivated her passion for advocacy and social justice.

Melinda has over 13 years of experience in a variety of settings and with diverse clients, including both long-term and brief interventions. Areas of expertise include: Children and adolescents with behavioral and sexual issues, anxiety and depression (including postpartum depression), relationship challenges: couples and families, and life stresses and next steps.

Melinda graduated from the Grambling State University in Grambling, Louisiana with her bachelor's degree in Social Work. She has a master's degree in Social Work from Our Lady of the Lake University in San Antonio, Texas. Melinda will be completing her doctorate degree from Capella University in Social Work in December with final approval.

Melinda is also continuously seeking to gain more skills and broaden her education. Melinda believes that change happens when people are given the guidance they need to draw on their own strengths and realize their potential to live fulfilling, happy lives.

Melinda provides an environment of compassion and support to help individuals and families overcome obstacles to move forward and thrive.

'You Entertain it, You Become It'

-Andrea Francis, CRMA/CPT, CYC-p

WITH GROWTH COMES WISDOM

I was born the only child of a *child*. My mother was a young girl confused; she didn't know what a young mother was supposed to do to provide for a child. The only meaning of mothering that her elders had given her was to provide materialistic possessions, but Momma did not believe that; she knew there was more she had longed for in life. It wasn't enough for her to just be told she was loved; she needed to feel the love.

Momma went out looking for the love; she felt that the gifts and money that she was given were love, that and helping to provide for her only child. Momma said no one ever questioned why men gave a little teenage girl gifts and monies, but she was degraded by family, who was supposed to protect her from these horrible manipulative men. Trying to own up to the "providing" image she was taught led to my momma experiencing things that no girl should have to entertain.

At a very young age my momma would tell me of my greatness, not to entertain the negative words of strangers, and not to entertain negative behaviors of friends and family, not just because I was her child, but I was her only child. My momma would do this daily. Letting me know how beautiful and smart I was, along with how I was so independent, courageous, and strong. She would sometimes describe my normal girls' life as if it were a way of life she had only dreamed of.

My momma did all this while being addicted to drugs and alcohol for years.

She would explain to me how the drugs and alcohol were not good for her and it had destroyed her life. Momma would also express how she was sorry she had to use drugs. I remember as a little girl sitting in one room while drug abuse went on in the next room. My momma would tell her fellow addicts about their greatness, even to the extent of listing their good qualities. I would listen and think about how dumb it sounded to hear an addict encourage another addict. I was too young to realize that the positive energy she was putting out would, in the future, encourage her to become clean and sober.

My momma was ashamed of how she had to *provide* for us, and how she struggled with the drug and alcohol abuse. I remember my momma coming home crying for help; she had again spent the monthly welfare check, which was only enough to pay the rent and utilities, on drugs. She cried out to this person about how she needed help to stop using drugs and alcohol. This person she had gone to for help only knocked her down more, belittling her by calling her a bitch and lil hoe. He advised her to get help from the old men who were already taking advantage of this young girl. I would constantly hear negative things about the young woman who always uplifted her only child. I heard over and over how my momma did not listen.

I was often compared to my momma as if I were her sibling. I was called the pretty one, smart one, but big one as if it was a communicable disease. I sometimes felt as if I had taken my momma's place as her mother/child. With this feeling I carried big burdens. I decided to be better than my mother but I didn't want to go against the grain because it was imperative for me to not change who I was as an individual.

My momma was so adamant about me finishing school, I knew I had to. But the burden of being like my mom was always thrown in my face and my mom's younger sisters' faces by teachers. We were constantly reminded that the only good things we could accomplish was to not get pregnant young, find a man who would take care of us and any kids we would have, and become a servant to the men in our lives. This was glorified as the best thing that could happen for us. Needless to say the "big one" met and married the first person that came along and showed some interest. The "big one" did not get showered with gifts or praised on my beauty or brains, just accepted by this person and his family. Don't get me wrong I learned so much from them and I am so grateful for that. But I know I married to release the burden from my momma. I felt I had to constantly do what my mother had not done, along with proving that my momma was courageous, beautiful, and independent and had also created greatness.

I was stuck between people pleasing and helping those who were really in need. Yes, unfortunately I had disregarded all my own desires. I was living numb. It is said that people go through the motions; I had lived most of my young life people pleasing. I put out what was expected of me all the time. I was often asked how I could be so understanding. People thought that nothing ever bothered me. But the truth was I was just numb to my own feelings. I feel like I became that way to protect my mom and myself from the negative comments. The "big one" had entertained the negativity for so long, I felt like I did not have an opinion. I was what they call a "GOAT" these days, someone who had everything someone wanted. They would come and get what they needed from me without having to put in work. But I thought that was how it was supposed to be.

Many moons later the only child became a mentor to teen moms. I had slipped into the role of the protector, preacher, and in some manner, a provider for these other little lives. Early on, I was very drawn to this career. It was like every teen that walked into the doors had a piece of my momma's story with them. I would often go to my momma with my frustrations about my job, she would say, "Ondria them lil girls don't have nobody, Momma used to be just like that, they need you!"

For over 10 years Momma's sober words kept me preaching to these girls. When Momma passed away, I began to listen to what I was expecting from these teenagers, which was to strive for excellence and always know your own worth. As a grown woman I was living numb and people pleasing; I was a hypocrite.

On one shift, like many shifts, I sat and talked to the teen moms along with a coworker I often referred to as Crazee Lady. Not in a negative tone, I think I had never been around a person who spoke the blunt truth at the drop of a dime. Crazee Lady spoke to the moms about their future. As many of them doubted that their future was promising, she encouraged them to change their current way of thinking, and to change the group of friends they entertained. As she spoke to them there were a few who became oppositional stating that it would not change their outcome in life; others felt it was possible. This amazing young lady watered the seed my momma had planted but so many others had prevented from growing. I had begun to be exposed to positive energy. A different way to give back and help others along with helping myself. Now I was being preached to and protected.

I refuse to carry the burdens of my elders, but I will continue to help those who feel they can't be helped.

I was placed in that environment to grow the seed my momma had already planted in me. I was now being protected, provided for, and preached to by this crazee lady and the teen moms I was placed there to do the same for. I knew I had found the love my mom had spoken to me about years ago. The love she was longing for. So, I decided to first better myself. A month after my mom passed way, I reenrolled in school and I became a certified medical assistant. This afforded me a position in the medical field that I had attempted for many years to complete. This action made the people closest to me upset, so I changed that group of friends. I began to live in my truth but expressing my feelings made me lose more friends and family. Then more of my momma's words kicked in. I was independent; all I needed was my faith. I knew I had My God on my side and anything was possible. A little secret, the greatest things that have happened in my life were NOT planned, and it was NOTHING I had dreamed of. All the things I entertained in my life I have definitely become, in some form.

About the Co-Author

Andrea Francis, CRMA/CPT, CYC-p, is a 47 y/o mother of 4 young men. She is currently employed as a Clinical Navigator by a healthcare agency. Though she has had a successful career, Andrea decided to continue her education. She is currently studying for her bachelor's degree. As an only child of a teen mother, she spent a vast amount of time isolated and reading. Some of her fondest memories include lying at home reading books by amazing women with the hopes of one day impacting the women in her life.

Over ten years ago her hopes became a reality when she was employed as a Youth Care Advocate. During her time of employment, Andrea was able to serve as a role model to not only the youth of her community, but she inspired her co-workers as well.

She was a listening ear and an advocate who provided sound advice. More importantly, she found her voice in a world where she once felt voiceless. Though her career has flourished, her focus remains the same. Andrea's desire is to help those who truly feel that they can't grow from past circumstances and those less fortunate to find their own way. No matter what.

'To Edify, Equip and Enlighten'

-Dr. LaTracey McDonald

THE MISSION TO STRIVE—*UNAPOLOGETICALLY US*

As a black woman in the publishing industry I've noticed that many are jumping on the *Self-Published Author* bandwagon without proper knowledge and wherewithal to promote and sell in the marketplace. I had to reach into the abyss of social media to stand out amongst the giants of Amazon, IngramSparks, Lulu and more to edify, equip, and enlighten Black authors in a space where they felt safe.

In business, it is essential for clients to like, know, and trust you. Now, multiply that by 100 when dealing with Black people. We struggle with trusting people especially with our money. So, being a Black woman that has written several books and been quite successful in the marketplace, I said "Yes" to God when I was given the vision to start Black Authors Rock. With my amazing team, we had to combat against every stigma that people have, not just 'Black Writers'.

I can publish for free on Amazon, so why would I pay your company to assist me with anything?

My cousin Pookie can read and they can edit my book, so why do I need to pay an editor for it?

Unrealistic for those in the publishing industry, but the reality in the thought process for many when entering into this arena of becoming a published author.

It begins with the mindset change. This is larger than just writing a book and selling it to your family and friends. Lack is a state of being. The definition is "absence, want; shortage, deficiency," and yet it is what it is. This is a difficult trial to combat. But, unapologetically, we did just that at Black Authors Rock. This is the mindset that we overcome daily as we equip Black writers to stand proud in the marketplace. To edify them to invest in the level in which they desire to circum. While enlightening them to be okay with being successful as a Published Author without regret.

Teaching them to stop apologizing for who they are. As well as to stop downplaying the greatness that lies in their melanin and stop trying to blend in. Yea, I said it. Stop tiptoeing around the fact that you are a **BLACK Author**!

We will be seen!

We will get paid!

We walk in abundance!

People will purchase our books daily!

Listen, there are too many spaces in the world where our Blackness is a problem, a weapon, an excuse; so this is a space where we are going to be *Unapologetically Us*! We have shied away from our Blackness for too long. We have tiptoed around our culture, around our heritage, around our ethnicity—all in order to make others feel comfortable. We cannot and will not do that any further—especially in our writing. ***Our Blackness is our reality***. We need not repress who we are and what we are, in order to gain the acceptance of those not like us. We are our own societal norm.

We stand out without even trying—so stop trying. At Black Authors Rock (B.A.R.), we can be our true selves, authentic to our Blackness, unapologetic in our stance. You do not fit in, Dear Aspiring Black Writer, Author, Storyteller, or Poet; we don't want you to fit in. You are a **Black** Author, and you Rock. We will not shy away from telling our stories, from giving our narratives, from letting it all be told in the fullest of our ethnic and cultural expression. We are us, and we will walk in the fullness of being us.

The day we individually and collectively decided to embrace who we are, our creativity, and all that comes with being Black men and women was the day we were set free from the fear of judgment. Once we all did it individually, we were able to begin to truly create what we wanted not just for ourselves but for *Black Authors Rock.*

It hasn't been easy being triumphant in this journey because people have an expectation of Black owned businesses that supersede what effort they offer and yet excellence is our goal.

We ARE Black Authors Rock! Illuminating those who aspire to inspire OUR community, to influence OUR people, and to make a global impact, which uplifts each of "US" in every way.

About the Co-Author

Dr. LaTracey, a known Professional Writers Consultant, edifies, equips, and enlightens aspiring writers to become published authors. She's the Chief Executive Officer, Publisher, and Founder of Black Authors Rock. She leads the Black Authors Rock online community for aspiring writers and authors, and is the Founder of Capstone Experience, Inc. Dr. LaTracey has a Masters in Nonprofit Management and Executive Leadership from St. Thomas University and an Honorary Doctorate of Humanitarianism from Global of International Alliance. She is an ordained Minister, licensed to preach the Gospel of Jesus Christ, specializing in youth ministry. In addition to her ministry gifts and talents, Dr. LaTracey possesses a profound skill set in Desktop Publishing, Business Development, and Motivational Speaking.

Dr. LaTracey passionately coaches authors through the publishing and promotion process that produces satisfying results and profitability from their literary works.

Connect with Dr. LaTracey in her private Facebook Group today: bit.ly/BlackAuthorsRockFB

www.BlackAuthorsRock.com

'Be Led by Your Dreams and Awaken by Your Passion'

-Lynette Edwards

DON'T DESPISE HUMBLE BEGINNINGS

At the young age of nine years old, I remember attempting to sleep in the middle of the night with a blanket slightly covering my face. The door opened and a familiar voice in a calming tone said, 'those poor children'. Looking up I saw flashes of police lights and a paramedic truck yet had no idea what transpired. The next morning I awoke to find my dad sitting on the sofa looking distraught; my mom had a nervous breakdown.

It was the first breakdown, but unfortunately not the last. Life went from great to strange in a matter of days. We went from living in a nice home with two parents, each with a good job and their own vehicle to living in the home of my grandparents with my dad.

Every weekend while the other kids played games and rode bicycles, we (my sisters, dad, and I) took a long trip to a state facility to visit my mom. A few weekends turned to months then, without notice, years. She never was quite 'right' after that first breakdown.

Unable to keep employment, drive a car, and function without medication, she went from living the normal carefree life of a wife and mother to a twenty-five-year battle with the thoughts in her mind. Thoughts that often instructed her to hurt her own children, fight family members, and make her feel as though she was alone; life's struggles can be cruel.

My dad took the role of both mother and father. Leaving a job that provided any and everything we wanted to settling for employment that 'kept the lights on'. We lived in public housing, were on food stamps, and had to adjust to the 'new norm'.

As time passed, we realized that we were blessed, not materialistically, but blessed in love. Family was there every step of the way and we made it. My dad was able to give my sisters and I the stability and love we needed while ensuring that we did everything we could to assist my mom on her heart wrenching journey.

My sisters and I grew older and wiser to life's circumstances at an early age. When we became young adults, we took the lead with 'taking care of mom' and being there for dad.

Then the unthinkable happened. There was a car accident and within moments my stability was gone; dad had died. As if that wasn't enough, a few short years later my mom was diagnosed with stage four cancer. Her sickness was so severe that within five months, in front of my eyes, she transitioned from this life.

Now what? Where do I go from here?

When life happens, we have two choices:

1. Give in and give up

2. Get up and get moving

With tears in my eyes, I chose to fight for my life. Fight to be better than the day before and fight to make something out of what appeared as nothing.

My voice seemingly came from written words. Something happened when I opened a computer screen; I soon realized that though I don't consider myself to be a traditional writer, I am able to write as a way of coping with my emotions. For years I have been able to publish books that aim to inspire, uplift, and encourage others on their journey.

From tackling tough topics to writing daily devotions, I was able to manifest a life for me that not only gave me freedom but allowed me to reach others who are in desperate need of inspiration. I have learned that in order to be a woman who leads, you must be a young lady who understands what it is to follow. Often times we want to 'be the boss' without knowing what it takes to lead as one.

For years I have followed and observed. Following has taught me:

1. It's okay to be silent

2. Never judge someone by a bad day

3. Wisdom comes in many forms

4. There is only one you; use it to your advantage

5. Girls who dream grow up to be women who lead

Giving up is not an option for me, nor should it be for you. Life has a way of 'waking' us up. For me it was through a heartbreaking upbringing, for others it differs. One thing that is for sure is that life is what you choose to make it.

Perhaps your desire is not to 'save the world' or 'influence a generation' but surely there is something worth fighting for.

I dare you to fight.

Fight for your daughter.

Fight for your sister.

Fight for the little girl inside of you that is screaming for better days.

Fight for your grandmother who never had the opportunities you have had.

Fight for the child patiently waiting for someone to lead her.

But most of all, fight for you!

You matter! Look in the mirror, what do you see?

There are gifts inside that only you possess waiting to be developed. You have the power to unwrap those gifts and bring forth what this world has never seen. There is only one you. Find your *why*! What makes the hair stand on the back of your head? What gives you purpose in the midst of life's storms?

You owe it to yourself to become an unstoppable force. While 'becoming' is difficult we have to eliminate the thoughts of fear and failure. Fear may be described as an unpleasant emotion, while failure can be identified as simply not having success in the eyes of the world.

Though the two words differ, they often go hand in hand, as unpleasant emotions arise when we don't succeed. We are scared to fail. Therefore, we allow fear to set in not realizing that sometimes you have to fall in order to appreciate getting back up.

When we experience failure in life, as we all will in one season or another, we must understand that it is not the end. It is in those times that we must find our muse and use it as a source of guidance for when we are ready to try again. If we don't encourage ourselves and find inner strength, fear will settle in and it will be more difficult to move forward.

The first time I began writing I failed. I didn't fail at writing per se, but I failed at not understanding the process; not comprehending that it takes more than putting words on a paper to be an efficient writer. I didn't take time to learn the process. In the end, it cost me money and time; time which I can never recover.

I often sit and reflect on where I would be now if I allowed the fear of criticism or the agony of defeat and failure to take over me.

It's okay to fail! I have learned to use failure as a stepping-stone to greater things ahead. It is important to know that because far too often we see people who speak of success but seemingly forget one important detail. They forget to be transparent about their journey.

I urge you to discuss your journey. Embrace those times that you failed. It is not only about the amount of times you fall that is relevant. But it is also about the one additional moment you fought to get back up and rise to the occasion.

Get up and look fear in the face. Get up and allow your faith to take you places beyond your wildest imagination and greatest expectations.

What are you waiting for? The world awaits. No one can lead like you nor can any woman bring forth the gifts that sit patiently inside; release, let go, and allow yourself to be awakened by your dreams and led by your passion.

About the Compilation Author

Lynette Edwards is an award winning and accomplished best-selling author, who developed Writers Rock™ mobile app. Writers Rock™ was developed to provide a direct platform for writers, bloggers, editors, illustrators, story tellers, book clubs, and more while providing resources and information from all across the world. The app has multiple chat 'lounges', contests, and awards an annual scholarship. The app is currently available at the App store and the Google Play store.

Lynette is a CEO of a Certified Small and Emerging Business, Priceless Inspirations. In addition, she has published multiple books in four different genres (inspiration, urban fiction, self-help, children), and she has a motivational adult coloring book. Lynette first made national coverage after writing her book *Take Off the Mask*. A book that encourages people to embrace their own identity and freely live a life without fear of rejection. She later wrote books with the aim to target single Christian women in an effort to show them that though their path may be lonely at times, it is far better to walk with God than to run towards man.

The books tackled Christianity, singleness, celibacy, bad relationships, mental health, and life choices.

A year later, Lynette wrote *Birdie's Way*, a children's book about a child with mental illness; the book was written to address the impacts mental health has on children. Lynette's latest book release is *Ready.Set.Succeed.* an empowerment interactive journal filled with almost 200 pages of motivation, affirmations, and positive tips to help you on your journey in life. In addition, she founded We W.R.I.T.E. mentorship program to assist new and aspiring writers on their journey.

She is the instructor and founder of Ready.Set.Succeed. an online academy that offers mini-courses to help entrepreneurs on their journey.

Lynette manages an online store 'UnstoppableByLyn' (www.unstoppablebylyn.com). The online store was inspired by her self-help journal 'Unstoppable' and offers custom T-shirts, apparel, and journals.

Lynette has made several guest appearances and has been featured through the years on Lifetime TV, Sheen Magazine, News Break, Miami Times, Black News, iHeart Radio, Upwords International magazine, African Global and *Secrets of a Woman* stage play in South Carolina, to name a few. Regardless if it's serving as an executive producer of a stage play, traveling on multi-state book tours, or moderating, Lynette continues to spread motivation and remind others to always look beyond their flaws and be unstoppable.

THE ABC'S OF AN EFFECTIVE WOMAN WHO LEADS

A- Ability to know when it's her time

B- Boldness to walk past naysayers

C- Cautious of the words she speaks

D- Due diligence in decision making

E- Eager to help others

F- Follow before attempting to lead

G- Gracefulness that leaves an impression

H- Honesty

I- Imagination that goes beyond your dreams

J- Judicious in all circumstances

K- Kind with her words

L- Leadership abilities

M- Mindset to make money while leading

N- Never judgmental

O- Optimistic

P- Persistent

Q- Quality service at all times

R- Reliable

S- Strategic in business dealings

T- Tolerant but not a pushover

U- Understanding

V- Valiant

W- Willing to teach others the way

X- Xany, never lazy

Y- Yearning for a better tomorrow

Z- Zealous about the work she does

A. Ability to Know When it's her Time

Understanding your 'set' time is essential. Every woman begins her journey differently. Some ease along taking baby steps while others rise to the occasion and jump right into leading.

Regardless of the type of leader you are, know that your time is already pre-set. No need to rush; no need to fear; your time will come.

While you wait, clap for the next woman (you'd be surprised at what she can teach you) but never lose focus as your time will come. Be patient, steadfast, and understand that what is for you will happen in its perfect time.

B. Boldness to Walk Past Naysayers

"Who does she think she is?" "Her product isn't all that!"

Yes, you will hear negativity on your journey. Sometimes it comes from those closest to you while other times it's from a complete stranger. You have to understand that you/your work won't be for everyone. You can't let that get you down. Be prepared for the backlash but stand tall through it all, you will make it; you will succeed.

C. Cautious of the words she speaks

Today what you say may not even matter, it may seem that no one cares. But what happens when you have a business? When your customer service is a deciding factor in the business you have worked so hard to build? Words matter. The words may be forgotten and people may act as if they don't care, but the words you speak matter; think before you speak.

D. Due Diligence in Decision Making

Every decision matters. From the most critical to the smallest decision it may impact your life and cause questions within your leadership.

E. Eager to Help Others

How much further would we be if we were to lend a helping hand? The truth is even leaders become afraid. Afraid that a small gesture of help can lead to an unforeseen failure on their part or the person may do 'better' than them.

Help anyway. Whenever you can lend sound advice, help someone on their journey and remember when one woman wins, we all win.

F. Follow before attempting to Lead

You can't lead where you have not followed; how will you know the way?

Have you heard the saying, 'my mentor has a mentor'?

Those words are spoken by leaders who understand that there is always room for growth. We don't just wake up leading a tribe. First, we follow and learn, then with wisdom and knowledge combined, we begin to lead.

G. Gracefulness that Leaves an impression

I may never remember everything you tell me, but, if it caused me emotional thought, I will always remember how I felt when we spoke. Good or bad.

With that being said, be graceful. It costs nothing.

H. Honesty

'Liar, liar pants on fire'. It's such a funny phrase. But it's memorable just like a lie. People will remember when you lie. And it may affect those that choose to follow you on your journey.

Be honest. Fact check before you speak. Be able to repeat words that are truthful and speak in a manner that is truthful.

I. Imagination that goes beyond your dreams

Have you ever thought that what you imagine can become a reality?

Dream Big. Dream outside the box. Dream so big that it scares you. Don't limit yourself; dream big then manifest your dreams and create the reality you desire for your life.

J. Judicious in all circumstances

Don't pick and choose which situation is relevant. Take time to understand every circumstance and base your judgement accordingly. Someone is watching and waiting for you to be the leader they need.

K. Kind with her words

There is a time and place for everything and every word. People fight battles that you may never know. Be that rainbow at the end of the clouds. Be the woman that helps another up versus the one that pushes the next one down. Words hurt. Words matter. Words heal; be a healer in a world full of hurt.

L. Leadership abilities

Who told you that you can lead? What makes you think you have what it takes? You must first evaluate yourself. You must understand that leadership is not for everyone nor is it for the faint at heart. Only you know the abilities you possess; do you truly have what it takes?

M. Mindset to make money while leading

Money matters. Especially when you lead in business. Not everyone has a money mindset. Seek a financial advisor, mentor, or money coach; someone who can help take you to the next level financially. You don't have to be money motivated to understand the laws of making money while leading.

N. Never Judgmental

Judge not and you won't be judged; actually that saying is incorrect in plenty matters. The truth is you will be judged, sometimes harshly, but don't fall to the level of the one who judges you. Instead, rise to the occasion. Be the bigger person. There is nothing wrong with leaders who decide to take a higher path. In fact, those who follow often yearn for leaders who understand that it isn't the person that judges that they want to learn from, but instead the one who leads; you.

O. Optimistic

This journey is not always easy. There is a reason that leaders are far and few. You have to learn to stay hopeful in dark seasons, walk away from situations that don't help you grow, and more importantly, you have to stay focused.

P. Persistent

One common core value of a true leader is the ability to never stop. Regardless of what comes your way, you owe it to yourself to never stop. Those days may seem long and the road gets tough but stay the course. It isn't a timed race; it's a one woman show. You are that woman. Stay the course; win your race.

Q. Quality service at all times

How do you provide quality service? Simple. Take your time, tune out the crowd, and work to the best of your ability. Quality service is key. Quality business practices bring forth results.

R. Reliable

Be the type of leader that others can depend on. Be there to assist. Be there when you have given your word. Be a woman of your word.

S. Strategic in Business Dealings

Understand your target audience/followers/business partners. You don't owe it to anyone to work with everyone. Take the time to understand what is needed for your business to succeed. Know who you are working with and be sure your mission is in line with one another.

T. Tolerant but not a pushover

There is a fine line between being compassionate and allowing others to walk all over you. As a leader it is imperative that you fully understand the difference.

Stand your ground. Be firm. Know the principles you have and implement them accordingly.

U. Understanding

Unless you were born with a silver spoon in your mouth, you understand what is required to be a great leader. Don't lose sight of the fact that we are all on different levels. Not everyone has mastered your area of expertise.

Be a listening ear and understand from your perspective.

V. Valiant

To be valiant is to show courage. As a leader you need courage.

Courage to take a stand. Courage to lead the way. Courage to speak when it seems that no one is listening. Courage to be the voice of reasoning, courage to push your way through.

W. Willing to Teach Others the Way

Being an effective leader requires paying it forward. Don't be so quick to forget those left in the back rooms awaiting their turn.

When you get the opportunity, help someone else on their journey; show another woman the way. Allow her path to be paved from the journey you have already traveled.

X. Xany, never Lazy

Get up! Who wants a lazy leader?

There is work to be done. Someone somewhere is depending on you; take a break if you must rest and unwind, but don't get complacent in the work that you do. You must stand tall and remain true. Someone needs you, someone cares, don't you stop now; get up and get going; finish strong.

Y. Yearning for a Better Tomorrow

What would have happened if every woman who led before you quit? How would that have affected you today?

Foresee what you want your daughter, niece, and female friends to witness in their lifetime. Yearn for more than what you see today. You can't give up. Not now, not ever. You owe it to the little girl inside to reach for the stars, hang on the moon, and be a force in the world.

Z. Zealous about the work she does

Allow your desire for your passion to shine through. Don't fear the unknown. Instead, walk in victory believing that you have what it takes to overcome defeat.

You are a voice in this world. You have what it takes to lead.

Be fierce in your endeavors and allow your work to speak for itself.

Own who you are and, more importantly, own what you bring to the table.

WOMEN LEAD

We hope this book has helped you on your journey. Reflect on the stories of how these women pressed through and on the ways they manifested their dreams. Remember the ABC's of leadership in all that you do.

You have what it takes. You will succeed; you simply have to focus and believe.

Despite where you are on your journey, one thing is for sure, women across the world are leading; heels are optional.

Reflections:

_____
_____
_____
_____
_____
_____
_____
_____
_____
_____
_____
_____
_____
_____
_____
_____
_____
_____
_____
_____
_____
_____
_____
_____
_____
_____
_____

WOMEN LEAD, HEELS ARE OPTIONAL...

WOMEN-LED BUSINESSES:

TRISTAN JACKSON- TJ INSPIRES

WWW.TJINSPIRES.COM

LEONA CARTER- CARTER STRATEGIES, LLC

HEYCOACHCARTER@OUTLOOK.COM

JASMINE KELLY-STEPHENS- JASMINE STEPHENS WELLNESS, LLC

JASMINE@JASMINESTEPHENSWELLNESS.COM

SHEENA YUTUC ADARAYAN- DIGITAL PRIORITY SOLUTIONS

HTTPS://DIGITALPRIORITY.SOLUTIONS

QUEEN AMUNUMHE- QUEEN'S FRAGRANCE AND STORE

AMUNUMHEQ@GMAIL.COM

AISHA WATTS- WATTS TRAVEL AND ADVENTURE

AISHAWATTS.INTELETRAVEL@GMAIL.COM

MADIHA JAMAL- THE CONTENT UNLIMITED

MADIHA@THECONTENTUNLIMITED.COM

WOMEN LEAD

www.ingramcontent.com/pod-product-compliance
Lightning Source LLC
Chambersburg PA
CBHW050511210326
41521CB00011B/2414